The Illuminas
The Light Centers of The Light Body

Written By Cheryl Banfield

Cover Illustration by
Graphic Designer Bryan Dechter

Illustrations by
Energy Artist Emily Medri

BALBOA.
PRESS
A DIVISION OF HAY HOUSE

Interior Graphics/Art Credit: Energy Artist Emily Medri

Balboa Press books may be ordered through booksellers or by contacting:

Balboa Press
A Division of Hay House
1663 Liberty Drive
Bloomington, IN 47403
www.balboapress.com
1 (877) 407-4847

Print information available on the last page.

ISBN: 978-1-5043-5818-7 (sc)
ISBN: 978-1-5043-5819-4 (e)

Balboa Press rev. date: 09/16/2016

Table of Contents

Love and Gratitude

I am deeply blessed with the presence of Sacred Lady Mary. I am equally as blessed with the beautiful spirits who have joined me on this journey of Love and Light. I give gratitude to these amazing spirits who are with me each day in love. I give deep love and gratitude to my husband, Robert, my daughter, Emily and my son, Calvin. I was able to accomplish this work in togetherness through the dedication of your work, love and support.

Preface

We are given opportunities in our lives to bring about positive change; sometimes these opportunities are traumatic events. I was given an opportunity in 2001. It was the new millennium, a time to celebrate letting go of the old and bringing in the new. I was ready for change but didn't realize the extent of change I was inviting into my energy, especially because I thought my life was fine. Though I was aware of using intuitive/psychic abilities since childhood, I did not foresee the universe was about to hit me over the head to awaken me. Fate, along with choices, catapulted me from a mild traumatic brain injury due to an ice skating fall, to an extraordinary life-changing journey.

I was blessed; what seemed to be traumatic life upheaval offered a new way of being. This experience led me to find myself and change my career to support others on their path. I realize I had disregarded many subtle opportunities or clues that could have brought about this life change more smoothly. Now I try to pay attention to the subtleties of clues and messages that are Divinely guiding, allowing my path to unfold more peacefully.

Many people have traumatic experiences to "awaken" them to their true path and to have a better understanding of who they are and why they are here on this Earth. There are easier ways to recognize the more subtle opportunities and to be able to utilize them for awareness. I discovered energy healing during my brain injury recovery. I began releasing past patterns, emotional blocks, and limiting behaviors. I opened to an expanded awareness of myself and of the world around me. I found energy healing to be a natural way to work with the whole body, and am able to share this gift with others. Energy healing has provided deeper and quicker opening and releasing, as well as support and Divine guidance through life transitions. It has been a miracle work.

In 2010, I began receiving information from Sacred Lady Mary and Archangels Gabriel, Raphael, Michael, Uriel, Ariel and Metatron for a new energy healing modality. The modality, which is called LoveLight Illuminations, helps raise the vibration and supports the development of the newly evolving human light body. The information provided was detailed and included an explanation of the structure of our new evolving light field.

Sacred Lady Mary has asked me to write this book to share the detailed information about our newly evolving light field. She has provided clarity of the new light centers that make up the structure of this new light field. Working with these new light centers, also in other modalities, helps raise the vibrational frequency of the Earth. Working with the light centers has been an amazing transformational experience. This work has the potential to quickly open others to Divine awareness within self and change their lives to live with peace and joy.

Divine awareness, whether it is of self or of life and the universe, can lead to trust, faith, a higher level of understanding, and peace and joy. Most of us are seeking more peace and joy, not only for our own benefit, but also for others and for this planet.

Many blessings and love to all of you on this journey of greater awareness and understanding, and finding peace and joy in every day.

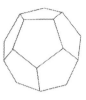

Introduction

This book is channeled from Mother Mary. I will refer to her as Our Sacred Lady Mary, per her request for this book.

Our Sacred Lady Mary is supporting the human journey of the spirit. She is present for comfort and available to assist; we simply need to ask for her assistance. She is encouraging all of us to open to our Divine love and light within. In this book she provides information for quicker evolvement and rising of our vibration with our spirit.

We are evolving spirits in a physical body. After the Earth's energetic shift in 2012, we are now able to live through our spirit and hold the higher Divine vibration. Moving into our newly developing light body means living in the higher vibration of our spirit in this physical experience. Living from our spirit means we can live in each moment in Divine grace, love, and light in the consciousness of Divine oneness.

This book shares an understanding of the structure of this newly evolving light body, what it means, and how to work with it. The light body consists of newly forming light centers. Information is provided in regards to how the light centers enhance wellness, and support us during energetic shifts in our vibration as we evolve with our spirit.

It is important to know that this book holds high vibrational energy. It may be experienced on many levels. Simply reading this book can raise your vibration and be a transformative experience. It can be calming and a bit heavy feeling; this means your vibration is shifting. If you are open to receiving this energy, you can shift energetically and heal on many levels of mind, body, and spirit.

The energy of this book holds a high vibration that our bodies are generally not accustomed to in this plane. Symbols of dodecahedron shapes are placed on each page to help balance your energy with the high vibration while reading. In sacred geometry, dodecahedrons represent the energy of the universe. The dodecahedron is also the shape of your new crystalline light centers forming in your light field.

You can experiment with the energy of the book by reading a page while covering the dodecahedron symbol. Notice how you feel with it covered, compared to when the symbol is visible. Some people who are sensitive to subtle energy may feel a significant difference while others may experience subtle sensations. Some of the sensations may be light-headedness or an out of body feeling. This is not harmful; it just makes it challenging to be conscious of what you are reading.

Vibrational meditation exercises are provided at the back of the book. They are quick and simple, yet powerful and energetically expansive. The meditations hold a high Divine vibration that is also healing.

Enjoy the magical experiences while reading this book and the many blessings it has to offer!

Evolving In Our Light

Our light is the light of our spirit. We hold the light of our spirit within ourselves. Our light is available and can be brought into our awareness in each moment. When we are aware of our light within, we can energetically shift and interact with the world around us through a positive and lighter perspective. We can actually feel the difference and desire to create positive experiences more often.

Creating positive experiences is easy by simply changing how we feel. When we choose a view from a positive perspective and allow time for understanding, we can feel happier. This creates an energetic shift. As our energy becomes lighter and happier, we attract a similar vibration. Positive experiences become more frequent. We can bring about change when the vibration of our energy is higher. Higher vibrations emit positive energy with the highest vibration being love. Awareness of our light within, which is our Divine love, raises our vibration, creating positive energy in the world around us.

We are in a physical body experience and are able to evolve with our spirit. We are evolving spiritually, opening our awareness to a deeper sense of our spiritual self. You may notice more people are using their intuitive abilities, seeking energy healing, and complementary modalities for health and wellness. People are awakening their medium-ship abilities to communicate with passed loved ones, angels and guides. Many people are looking for ways to develop their own intuitiveness and Divine gifts. When we expand our light, we can use our own abilities at higher levels of consciousness, beyond what we have experienced in this human existence in the past.

It is time for us to move beyond our mindfulness of our awakened state and step into living through our spirit in each moment. Living through our spirit allows us to interact with our environment and others from our Divine place of love and peace. We can deepen our awareness and understanding of our true being by energetically shifting into our spiritual vibration, or evolving into our light body. When we blend the energy of our physical and spiritual self, we can experience ourselves from a higher level of consciousness. Through our spiritual self we are able to master a deeper understanding, balance emotions, and realize our true intentions, making it easier to shift our perspective. We can awaken with understanding, allowing healthier interactions with others and our environment, bringing peace and joy in our daily lives.

Living through our spirit allows us to interact with our environment and others from our Divine place of love and peace. As our vibration rises, we expand our light energy and in turn expand our awareness and the way we experience life. We are able to experience beyond our six senses and open to a physical experience filled with peace, love and joy.

As peace, love and joy begins within each of us, individually we can play an integral role in bringing peace, love and joy to this planet.

Beyond The Chakras: Our Newly Evolving Light Field

As of December 2012, the vibration in the Earth's atmosphere holds a higher vibration. It was a tipping point and opening for new expansion. The evolving Earth had shifted to a high enough energetic frequency that allowed an increased rate of energetic expansion. This also allowed our energy fields to expand more easily. Since then, we have begun developing new energy centers called light centers or illuminas. These light centers are beyond the chakras and located in the outermost part of our energy field, our light field.

These new light centers, illuminas, make up our newly evolving crystalline light body. Our new light field regulates the amount of radiance of our spiritual light. Our light field allows the higher vibration of our spirit to be held in this physical Earth experience. The structure can hold and regulate the higher vibration of our spirit, which allows us to transform our experience as a human being living with more of our spiritual energy.

Our physical bodies are running at a much lower vibration than our spiritual energy. Our bodies can only handle a gradual increase in vibration. Bringing more of our spiritual light into our energy affects the body. The physical body shifts in energetic frequency as we evolve with our spirit. We can experience physical fatigue, body aches, insomnia and several other symptoms when our body is adjusting to the higher vibration.

Our body needs time to adjust. This new light field helps our bodies adjust gradually to the higher vibration as we bring more of our spiritual self into this plane.

The Earth's vibration is also rising. As the vibration rises on Earth, balance with spirit is essential. Connecting with the Divine within self balances our inner world and outer world. We influence the outer world as we raise our own vibration and by being in balance with our spirit.

The light centers hold the higher vibration of Divine light and are spiritual light centers associated with bringing our spirit into the Earth experience. The light centers are energy centers different from chakras. Chakras are energy centers associated with our physical experience as a spirit, while the light centers allow us to hold more of our spiritual energy. Holding more of our spiritual energy allows for quicker evolvement with our spiritual self in this physical plane. We can think of this process as ascension on Earth, evolving ourselves into our full spirit within this human experience. These new light centers are also different than chakras in form and in their functioning. The light centers are crystalline in form and can hold high vibrating Divine frequencies of light. Each light center represents different aspects of evolving into our spiritual self.

The light centers are new energy areas for healing and enlightenment as we ascend into a more blended spiritual/physical experience. They allow balance in all areas of our physical being as our vibration rises, and ease in evolving with our spirit. These new light centers allow us to open to our spiritual awareness and experience our Divine gifts with balance and grace.

These centers support our body as we elevate our vibration, allowing us quicker spiritual growth and deeper healing. Through these new light centers we can access higher vibrating energy to support our expanded awareness, higher consciousness, and our spiritual abilities. We have a direct alignment with our spirit within and connection to all in Divine oneness.

With the support of Divine energies and our willingness to surround ourselves with higher vibrating energy, we are able to evolve these centers more quickly. We can expand our light centers through positive thoughts and intentions, as well as by coming from a place of love and kindness. Being in contact with the higher vibration expands the light centers. We can also expand them through any of the healing arts that work with mind, body, and spirit.

Expanding in our light can bring about powerful life change. As our light expands we can bring wellness and transformation to the world. Together, the illumination of our light can bring humanity into an awakened state of peace, understanding, and love, while also creating wellness and transformation for the world.

The Structure of Our New Light Field

Our new light field is the outermost layer of our energy field and holds our new evolving crystalline light body. Our light body allows our spiritual light into this Earth experience more than ever before.

The Illuminas

Our light body structure is made up of crystalline illuminas, light centers, which can hold the higher vibration of our spirit. Thirteen illuminas encircle the energy of our body from about 11 feet below our feet to about 12 feet above our head; they are all perfectly and vertically aligned. Illuminas are called light centers as they hold and radiate our spiritual light. These light centers are Earth plane sensors and connections/openings to our Divine self. Twelve illuminas (1st-12th) correspond to elements of healing for fully blending with our spirit, and one illumina (13th) is our gateway to the Divine plane. The illuminas are the general physical locations for the elements of healing for spiritual ascension. They can be expansive as they radiate our spiritual light.

Each illumina is in the shape of a dodecahedron. The illumina's dodecahedron shape represents the spiritual self and physical self. The 12 sides, each a pentagonal face, represent 12 energy centers called illums. These illums funnel into a point at the center of the dodecahedron. They look like vortices. The illums correspond to elements of healing: six are opening us to our spiritual energy in the non-physical existence, and six are grounding us in our spiritual energy.

The Illums

The 12 Illums (energy centers) of the Illumina:

The first six illums are of the physical energy of the body and are related to aspects of the physical attributes:

1 — Unos Illum — Magnetism (cohesiveness) with others
2 — Deco Illum — Relativity of self in environment
3 — Ideil Illum — Electrical currents (energetic alignment)
4 — Jie Illum — Interpretation of self in relation to surroundings
5 — Lepal Illum — Motion/movement (action – expression of self)
6 — Nano Illum — Emotions with awareness/understanding

The second six illums are of the spiritual energy of the body and related to the spiritual attributes:

7 — Septo Illum — Sensual integration of knowing all
8 — Canto Illum — Memory and awareness stored
9 — Dondo Illum — Expansiveness of self
10 — Sentra Illum — Relay of thought and communication (SENTRA -Sedentary Epoch Noise Tuning RILR {Realistic Investigative Light Relationship} Activity)
11 — Illio Illum — Interrelations and awareness of beyond this Earth experience, blending experiences in all dimensions
12 — Manto Illum — Compassion — Love with Divine understanding

Each illum holds aspects of physical and spiritual attributes allowing energy work for deeper release and shifting. As each illumina has illums with the same attributes, they are interconnected and vibrational shifts can be shared between them.

Oples

Our light body is an organized system to regulate, control and manage the flow of light through and around the physical and energetic body.

Four light channels carry the light through and around the illuminas: two run through the inside of the illuminas and two surround the illuminas in the outer edge of the light field. These channels of light are called oples. The oples circulate Divine light through our crystalline light body.

The Mietor (Managing Internal and External Transmission Of Radiance) is the outer edge of our light body field that is made up of the Jo ople and IJo ople. These two oples carry the light around the illuminas surrounding our physical body, regulating the transmission of light. We can imagine our light field as a sphere around us, with the outer layer working in two ways: one way that emits our light, Jo ople, and the other that receives light, IJo ople, from Divine and others.

The Meatus (Managing Ethereal Alignment To Universal Source) Linaus (Lineal Intention Nourishing And Unifying Self) is a vertical energetic axis that runs through the center of the illuminas. The Meatus Linaus consists of the two light channels that run our Divine light through our illuminas from the 13th illumina to the 1st illumina. The Pelo ople flows light downward, while the Afino ople flows light upward with a continuously circulating flow. The light flows in and out of the lower part of the 13th illumina, which is called the Sea of Light.

Sea of Light

The Sea of Light is a neo-plasmic field in the lower part of the 13th illumina. This part of our light body structure is a holding area for energetic light information, which can be accessed by our higher self when needed for this Earth experience.

Celfmer

Below the Sea of Light is another area called the Celfemer (pronounced: chelfmer); it regulates the movement of light in and out of the illuminas by allowing the appropriate amount to travel into the Pelo ople and out the Afino ople. These oples are like rivers flowing in and out of the Sea of Light through the center of the human body. The light runs up and down the oples at the same time, creating a constant flow of Divine light through the body.

PIU - 13th Illumina

Our 13th illumina, named PIU (Pure Illumination of the Universe), is an evolved illumina. It is a sheer gateway between our life existence on Earth and our life existence in Source energy or the Divine plane. Our spirit transitions through this gateway from the physical body to the Divine experience.

Uepo - The Source Light Channel

The Source Light Channel above the 13th illumina is called Uepo (pronounced: oowaypo). This channel regulates the level or vibration of light energy entering through the gateway into the Sea of Light. This light channel maintains balance and allows the sufficient amount of vibration to enter the illuminas. As the body adjusts gradually to the higher vibration, more light flows into the Sea of Light. When the body adjusts to a higher vibration of light circulating through the 13 light centers, the centers expand with light, causing our vibration to rise.

Living in a Higher Vibration: Evolving The 13 Illuminas

These are exciting times as people come together seeking greater awareness to bring peace and love to this planet. The Earth's energy is shifting and humanity is awakening to a higher consciousness. We can experience simple pleasures with expanded awareness. Working with our newly evolving light centers can allow us to move more quickly into a life filled with joy.

Life can be a beautiful and peaceful meditation if we allow it to be. We often think of meditation as quieting our mind; however, meditation can be part of what is going on around us. Life can become a subtle meditation simply by a shift in awareness. We can be peaceful and joyful in our experiences of daily living.

Have you ever just sat for a few moments without purpose, doing nothing, just sitting there resting and allowing whatever was going to happen to just happen in that moment? For instance, have you watched a butterfly on a warm summer day just noticing it? Or do you remember a time that you sat on the edge of a pond and noticing a little group of minnows swim by, or standing by a river watching a leaf float by? In that moment you were in a subtle meditative state. In that moment you were "allowing." During moments like these we can recognize how simple it is just to be.

We can expand those moments in our every day life, pausing and experiencing in a calm and peaceful manner. Simply recognizing and pausing for awareness in any moment can shift perspective and create a meditative and peaceful experience.

We can bring this awareness of just being into our every day experience interacting with others. By having a sense of who we are as spiritual beings, we can maintain harmony in our energy. Blending with our spiritual self allows energetic wholeness and promotes a strong boundary for supporting our Divine vibration in all interactions.

We can expand our awareness: see the small in big, and the big in small. We can shift perspective to create desirable experiences. As we are Divine, our energy is part of everything. We can experience ourselves through others or other things. We can realize we are part of a flow of information; we can access Divine knowledge, have a sense of other existences, and recognize that all of our physical senses are matched by spiritual senses. We can recognize emotions as clues from our higher self that move us in a direction. Emotions can be held lightly in our energy, allowing an understanding of the bigger picture.

As our physical world view broadens, we can have an array of opportunities in creating and manifesting our reality.

We can create our own reality through the eyes of Divine self by seeing each moment as a blessing, and by experiencing from a place of peacefulness.

Being in our Divine light we can experience an expanded perspective, allowing Divine love to flow through each of our experiences. Evolving our illuminas allows us to hold more of our Divine light, lightening our energy and releasing us from the denser physical energy. The lighter our energy is, the easier we can shift our vibration and respond with joy in daily life.

By developing the illuminas we can evolve our Earth experience. The structure of the illuminas is our crystalline light body, our Divine form here on Earth. Evolving into this new form of a blended physical and spiritual existence, allows a new experience in the denser energy of the Earth plane. The illuminas allow the physical evolvement into the physical-spiritual form.

We can work with the illuminas to support spiritual growth and movement toward full spiritual radiance. The illuminas can be worked with through various techniques and energy healing modalities. Some techniques can be focusing with intention over particular illuminas, expanding, healing, or releasing energy through them. They are very easy to work with as they hold a higher vibration causing the energy to move quickly and easily. The illuminas are connected into all areas of the physical and energetic body including the chakras, meridians, and other systems.

The Illuminas are categorized as Physical Illuminas, Spiritual Illuminas and the Cosmic Illumina.

Illuminas 1-6 are the physical illuminas as they relate to the aspects of our physical existence. They provide a strong foundation for expansion, stability, alignment, and balance of our energies. They allow understanding and perspective in self-awareness and the sense of inner Divine self-love. These illuminas provide deeper integration and harmony of our physical and spiritual self in this physical experience.

Illuminas 7-12 are spiritual illuminas as they relate to aspects of our spiritual existence in this physical experience. They can open us to our true Divine being and expanded awareness of our relation to the Divine plane. They allow us to experience our spiritual qualities in this Earth experience and live in our Divine light.

The Cosmic Illumina - 13 is the meeting place of the physical plane and spiritual plane. This is our Divine gateway and opening to expanded Divine experiences.

The Physical Illuminas (1-6)

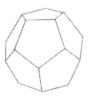

1st – Base Illumina / The Dais:
(area 11 feet below our feet)

The 1st illumina is the Base Illumina, also called the Dais. It is located about 11 feet below our feet. The 1st Illumina is the base of our crystalline light body. This illumina is considered our spiritual platform in the Earth plane for expanding in our spirit. It is associated with our foundation of spiritual strength and our Divine consciousness as a human being. This light center is an opening or gateway to other energies in the Earth plane and our expansiveness in this physical experience.

We can start with raising the vibration in our first light center. Starting with the first light center allows the development of the higher vibration of our spiritual form here in the Earth plane. We can move through first light center and access Divine for blending with the vibration of the Earth.

This illumina begins our transformation from being a human with a spirit to a spirit in the physical form. As our vibration rises, we hold more of our spirit's energy and abilities allowing us to begin interacting and experiencing the Earth from our spiritual perspective and attributes.

This illumina helps us with acceptance of our spiritual self and adjustment in evolving into a higher vibration in this Earth plane.

Evolving the first illumina heals aspects of ourselves to allow and accept we are spiritual energy with the ability to expand our perspective in the Earth plane.

2ⁿᵈ – Earth Illumina / The Radix:
(area 4 feet below our feet)

The 2ⁿᵈ Illumina is the Earth Illumina, also called the Radix. It is located about 4 feet below our feet. It is our link to being grounded in the Dais and Earth, and stabilizes our upper light centers aligning us in the Divine plane. This light center stabilizes all of our internal and external energies, and is supportive for our evolving ascension work aligning our energy with our Divine vibration. This light center is for aligning all of our spiritual and physical energy. It allows for alignment with the spiritual vibration of Pure Divine Love. Directing the energy in this light center in a structured grid can bring flow and ease, without disruption or blocks, and allow the connection of energetic links of the physical body to the spiritual body. Working with focus and intention over the second light center can bring this energetic direction and connection. Work over this light center by spinning it or circling over it to align energetic flow and connection. There is a magnetic pull for the highest vibration in this light center, allowing the spiritual and physical energies to flow and align.

By working with this illumina, we can experience stabilization in our energy in any situation. Our internal and external energies can be aligned, by simply imagining this area spinning. This technique provides a feeling of being settled in our energy. This also brings our energy into alignment with our true intentions and Divine direction, allowing us to be in the flow of our higher guidance.

Being in alignment allows a sense of things lining up for us. We can ease through transitions, simplify decision-making, and allow daily activities to Divinely unfold.

3rd – Balance Illumina / The Tetrad:
(area around our feet)

The 3rd illumina is the Balance Illumina also called the Tetrad. It is located around our feet. This is a physical and energetic sensor to relate to the Earth plane. It supports and balances our physical self with our spiritual self. This is an area that maintains balance for our physical energies as we evolve in our awareness of our spiritual self.

This illumina creates energetic balance with our spiritual and physical bodies. Working with this illumina opens awareness of a true sense of spiritual self, allowing a shift from the human experience into a more spiritual experience in physical form.

By evolving this illumina, we are tipping our vibration to live from a more spiritual vibration and approach life from that perspective for the human process, deepening Divine understanding, and dismantling belief systems we have previously lived by. We can walk on the Earth grounded in our spirit rather than grounding into the energy of the Earth. With the vibration of grounding in our spirit, we can help raise the vibration of the Earth. The Earth no longer needs to be the anchor of one's energy. We can blend in our spirit, anchoring in Divine to pull up the Earth's vibration where needed. We can allow ourselves to hold the higher vibration of our spirit fully present and available to assist the Earth as the Earth assists us, like a dance of vibrations with the Earth.

Balancing with our spiritual self supports our Divine work in the Earth plane. We are here to help the Earth shift and help others evolve. Being in our Divine light allows us to give as well as receive with grace and ease. Togetherness as one as we are in Divine Oneness moving this planet to the vibration of love and peace. We can be our Divine self in the energy of oneness.

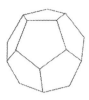

4th – Harmonious Illumina / The Exisensor:
(area around our knees)

The 4th Illumina is the Harmonious Illumina, also called the Exisensor. It is located around the knees. It is a connection to our external energies and a sensor of other energies in or around our energy field. This light center provides harmony in our own energy and in our energy in relation to other energies.

This illumina allows recognition of who we are as energetic beings and helps us maintain our energy in various experiences. This illumina allows us to maintain our energy harmoniously around various vibrations. It helps us shift and navigate in our energy as a spiritual being.

Working with this light center creates healthy energetic boundaries. It builds energetic wholeness and acts as a strong boundary of support of our Divine vibration in all interactions. It builds on the vibration of the first three light centers in relation to the blending of self with spiritual self. The fourth light center strengthens movement and navigation in each Earth experience with defined energy of self. This illumina helps us maintain self-energetic boundaries for wholeness and for allowing the full potential of our spiritual vibration, while maintaining the vibration of Divine oneness that we are not separate and are connected to all.

5th – Power Illumina / The Core Dais:
(abdominal area)

The 5th Illumina is the Power Illumina, also called the Core Dais. It is located around the abdomen and supports higher consciousness of self, self-empowerment, sense of self, and self-reflection. It is associated with our core intentions as we are awakening to our spiritual abilities and life path. This light center blends our spiritual and physical sensuality and higher awareness of our role in this physical existence. This illumina is an opening to discovery of our true nature.

Working with this illumina allows us to discover misinterpretations of experiences and the roles we played. The 5th illumina represents how we define ourselves by our experiences in the human plane rather than experiencing from our awareness of who we truly are as a Divine being. Misinterpreting experiences and defining ourselves based on our experiences creates energetic disruption within our energetic frequencies, blocking the flow of higher vibrations. This lowers our frequency and can deplete our nourishment from spirit, which leads us to becoming more "human" in our thinking and feeling disconnected from our true being and Divine source. This can bring further analytical thinking in alignment with disconnect from source, and the thinking of "I'm not worthy or not deserving or not capable," creating a pattern of this frequency. This is an example of how we can use this illumina to release these disruptive patterns by healing or shifting the frequency and thought analysis. Releasing to create a healthier thought pattern and frequency within allows higher vibrating experiences with Divine flow, and brings feeling supported in spiritual growth and expansion. Our true nature wants resolve. Reacting and lashing out is the act of trying to resolve for peace. Ultimately, all disruption is from within. We can heal over this illumina to bring ourselves into our core knowing we are perfectly Divine. We are not defined by this Earth experience. We are defined by the pureness of our Divine self.

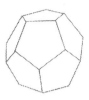

6th – Divine Illumina / The Helind:
(area around our chest and throat)

The 6th Illumina is the Divine Illumina, also called the Helind. The Helind is located around the heart and throat areas. It is associated with Divine self, which our Divine love and Divine truth. It assists with release of ego and expression of Divine self. This light center supports rapid transformation, the connection and awareness for Divine Love, and unconditional love of self and all in the universe.

We are love. Love is our basic building block. Humans are built on love: it is our true nature. Those who appear not to be of love are those who hold pain of feeling or perceiving a disconnection from love. In reality, no one is disconnected from love, as that is our spirit. Re-experiencing the connection of love allows the realization, understanding, and perception to shift. We can experience this connection with love humanly; however, to experience pure, Divine love humanly, we need to free ourselves from emotion and a sense of doing something in order to love. Love, pure Divine love, comes from our spirit. It is still, peaceful, expansive, and unconditionally flowing energy from within us. Divine love is our love for ourselves as our perfect spiritual energy. To allow love to flow, we must fill ourselves with this love and allow it to overflow and radiate to others and our surroundings. We can be the pure sense of Divine love in each moment. The energy flows subconsciously. The conscious mind can create a perceived disruption so we may not be aware of the feeling of experiencing the flow of Divine love flow. We can be aware of Divine love when we take the time to be still and present in a moment. We can allow awareness of our true nature flowing through us.

Working with this illumina provides deeper awareness in Divine self and healing for our energy to shift into a higher vibration for easier recognition and experiencing of Divine love.

The Spiritual Illuminas (7-12):

7th – Confluence Illumina / The Centrix:
(area around our head)

The 7th Illumina is the Confluence Illumina, also called the Centrix. It is located around the head. It is the central energetic meeting place of the mind, body and spirit, connecting the lower Illuminas with the upper Illuminas. This Illumina supports integration and balance of these three aspects of self for spiritual expansion and growth.

This illumina holds our crown and third eye chakras. It also holds an energetic area around our pineal gland that relates to our mind, body, and spirit integrated experience. Our 7th illumina is a transition point into our spiritual based illuminas. We are experiencing the human aspects from a spiritual viewpoint, whereas our lower light centers (1-6) are coming from the human viewpoint. As we work more with our upper light centers, we begin to experience our life from our spiritual perspective. We begin using our spiritual awareness as an approach to life and how we experience everyday interactions. We truly are spiritual beings, and the sooner we accept and embrace our true nature, the quicker we can evolve into joyful, high vibrating relationships with ourselves and all around us. We also can begin experiencing ourselves in an expansive perspective, recognizing we are more powerful than we realize. We have the ability to create our way of living and what happens to us. Being in the flow of our true nature influences everything that comes into our energy. This illumina moves us towards higher levels of awareness. Our experience in this plane is associated with our level of awareness. As our awareness is elevated and expanded, the more easily the lower 6 light centers flow.

Working with this illumina creates a shift in our vibration to transpose our way of being as human with a spirit to a spirit in human form. The emphasis becomes our spiritual way of being and approaching life's experiences. The mind begins to see from the spirit perspective, a broadened insight of love and expanse for situations. Deeper understanding is achieved through Divine insight versus our human senses. We can begin to incorporate spiritual interpretations to all of life's experiences and allow the concepts like "everything happens for a reason" or "there is more than we can see as to why things are happening." These concepts and others like them can be accepted into our energy with an expansive understanding, allowing, letting things be and going with the flow of everything unfolding. This helps us to take a step back from situations either knowing or trusting to let things happen Divinely and having a sense of when to take action rather than react. This illumina allows us to find greater peace within ourselves and with the world around us.

8th - Awareness Illumina / The Transpoint:
(area 1 foot above our head)

The 8th Illumina is the Awareness Illumina, also called the Transpoint. It is located about 1 foot above our head. It provides greater awareness of higher consciousness, clarity, and transparency of reality. It allows rapid awakening to universal harmony. This light center accesses past, present, and future, and provides the ability to operate in timelessness for healing and transforming.

This illumina lets our awareness expand. We can shift perspective to create desirable experiences. As we are Divine, our energy is part of everything. We can experience ourselves through others or other things. We can be anything between an expanded version of ourselves to an expanded version of the universe, to an even more expanded state of Divine Oneness. We can be everything and nothing all at once, nothing being a blend of just being with no identity. This is the highest vibration of what is just LOVE, Divine being, or flowing in just being. As we are all part of Divine, we are part of everything. We can realize we are part of a flow of information, have access to Divine knowledge, can have a sense of other existences, and that all of our physical senses are matched by spiritual senses. What we are in the physical, we are also in the spiritual. Our awareness of our spiritual senses allows us to experience our spiritual being in physical form. As our physical world picture broadens, we can have an array of opportunities in creating and manifesting our reality.

Working with this illumina allows a playful and expanded way of using our perspective and moving our energy. Allow an expanded perspective to see the small in big, and big in small. Shifting perspective can allow a sense of expansion of form to no form in reality. Sense being a part of the universe. We can be our true selves; our true love is present in past, present, and future. Our Divine love is constant, infinite, and timeless; this never changes. Time collapses with a sense of just being in our expanded energy. Raising our vibration through this illumina lightens our energy allowing fluidity. Fluidity provides no room for disruption within our energy and nothing is held onto. We can move through situations with grace and ease, peaceful in our Divine vibration.

9th – Wholeness Illumina / The Unilum:
(area 2 feet above our head)

The 9th Illumina is the Wholeness Illumina, also called the Unilum. It is located about 2 feet above our head. This illumina evokes wholeness of self in all of our essences. This Illumina is associated with connection to our higher self and interactions with higher self. It opens us to a higher state of consciousness and sense of connection with our true Divine being. This illumina brings us into living through our higher self.

Working with this illumina enhances our connection to our higher self in every day experiences. We can embrace our higher self for direction and guidance for the flow of everyday living. We can be our true self, the higher self in each moment. When we allow ourselves to walk each day with awareness and connection with our spirit, our insight becomes a blend of our human and our spiritual experience in this Earth existence. This illumina raises our vibration for our relationship with our spirit and moves us energetically to become one with our spirit. What we experience and how we experience it does not have to be separate from our spirit. With understanding and allowing an expanded perception, life can be an active spiritual experience with awareness of a level of peace, love, and joy. We have access to our Divine power. We are our own destiny. Establishing a relationship with self embraces the feeling of not being alone. In fact, you will find you never feel lonely. You may be alone, but not lonely. You have your Divine self.

10th – Telepathic Illumina / The Vistar:
(area 3 feet above our head)

The 10th Illumina is the Telepathic Illumina also called the Vistar. It is located about 3 feet above our head. It supports and opens us to our spiritual vision, telepathic and intuitive connection, and communication. This illumina expands insight and visibility, and allows a greater ease in communicating with angels and guides.

Working with this illumina raises our vibration for awareness of communication beyond this plane and to experience communication on all levels. It expands our abilities in the clair-essences for daily living. It opens us to the awareness that self is a Divine channel. Divine love and light flows through us in each moment. Light holds information of the universe. We are all energy connected to all energy. When we stay in our light we are aware as a Divine channel. We receive information in different ways through our spiritual senses and then filtered into our physical senses. Often we are acting humanly based on channeled information. This illumina opens us to higher frequencies by allowing our vibration to be high enough to receive higher frequencies. This allows clarity, channeling, and inter-dimensional information to flow with ease. We are expansive energy with access to all of the information in the Divine plane.

11th – Connection Illumina / The Daoli:
(area 4 feet above our head)

The 11th Illumina is the Connection Illumina, also called the Daoli. It is located about 4 feet above our head. It allows greater self-awareness and connection in all dimensions, planes, and all existences. It supports expanded awareness of multi-dimensional self, connections in other planes and dimensions, and a greater sense of oneness.

Working with this illumina allows a deeper sense of Divine connection. All in the universe is interconnected and expansive fluid energy runs through all. This light center allows the awareness of other dimensional realms, providing a feeling of connection with all. It brings awareness of self in other experiences, with an integration of the spirit for an expansion of self. There is no need to hold onto identity and create form. We can release and let all energy expand and move through without holding onto to anything in a specific focus. As all is in all, nothing is lost and everything just is.

Healing through this illumina allows a feeling of balance in this plane with our infinite spirit and being a part of everything. This illumina helps with resolve around death and moving on in our spirit, allowing our spirit to flow.

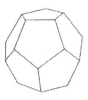

12th - Perceptual Illumina/ The Lumis:
(area about 5 feet above our head)

The 12th Illumina is the Perceptual Illumina, also called the Lumis. It is located about 5 feet above our head. The Lumis is an illuminating light center for Divine wisdom and Divine self. This Illumina supports a higher understanding of cosmic reality and perception. It is a connecting place of soul self and Divine oneness. This illumina accesses full recognition of Divine within self, realization of self, and sense of being in Divine oneness.

Working with this illumina can move us to full resolve in oneness with self. This allows full compassion, and understanding that all is an extension of self. Pure manifestation of reality is through Divine perception. We can create our own reality through the eyes of Divine self. Seeing each moment as a blessing, experiencing from a place of peacefulness not from emotion. We can expand into an awareness of dispersing the energy created in human interactions and allowing many experiences of love. The realization can be brought forth that in reality there is no lacking, as all is accessible and purely Divine. Human reaction (acting out of emotion) is trying to slow the movement of the energy in order to grab onto it, identifying it, as a way to know how to be, which creates disruption in flow and often blocks energy. Allowing an expansive space in awareness of human senses promotes release, a movement Divinely flowing for growth and direction, and natural healing. We can be in our Divine wisdom viewing our life experiences from a distance, bringing in the Divine perspective of this lifetime is just a moment.

The Cosmic Illumina (13):

13th - Cosmic Illumina / PIU
(Pure Illumination of Universe):
(area 12 feet above head)

The 13th Illumina is the Cosmic Illumina, also called the PIU, the acronym for our Pure Illumination of the Universe. It is located 12 Feet above head. This is the meeting place of the physical plane and Divine plane, and where we leave our physical body when we cross over into the Divine plane. This illumina also regulates Divine energy flowing through the illuminas.

This is the area of pure Divine love. Through this light center we can more readily access the PURE (Providing Universal Radiant Energy) state of being and cosmic connection of oneness. As Divine energy we are simply free from emotion, identity, beliefs and interpretations as we are simply Love. We are simply radiating Love, in the stillness and gracefulness of just being.

We can work with this illumina as our access or gateway to the spiritual plane where we fully blend our spiritual energy in Divine oneness. This allows purely radiating light within the nonexistence of space and time. We can behold the light of the universal cosmos. We can just be, beyond trusting in the unity of oneness not less than, not more than. We can be the Divine knowing that everything and nothing is in all, the wholeness of just being and all is Love. Divine Love is beyond a feeling or sensing. We can be resigned in self-truth, and in Divine knowing. Be rest assured we are one with God or Source or Divine Oneness, in resonance of the highest vibration and in creation.

Simple Meditations for Transformation

The following meditations are part of LoveLight Illuminations. LoveLight Illuminations is a healing system channeled and designed to work with the light centers for wellness and transformation. This modality has illuminating techniques and exercises that expand and support the new light centers. For more information you can visit the LoveLight Illuminations website www.lovelightilluminations.com.

These simple meditations offer the opportunity for powerful life change. Through these easy meditative exercises, your light centers activate your Divine healing light and expansion. Your vibration is raised more quickly for wellness and spiritual growth. Working with these meditations can speed up evolvement in your spirit. They can help you find deeper peace and love in yourself, which is then reflected in the world around you.

The meditations can be performed anytime and require very little effort. There is no need to try to quiet your mind. There is nothing you need to do, just simply allow a Divine experience. The effects can be subtle and can take time. Often those who work with them notice positive change within a couple weeks. You may want to try them a few times before you are aware of your experience.

There are three meditations: Opening to Your Divine Love Meditation, Connecting to Your Higher Self Meditation, and Expanding in Your Light Meditation.

Enjoy exploring your light centers!

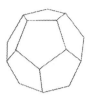

Opening to Divine Love Meditation

This meditation offers the opportunity to open to your Divine love of self. Opening to your love can create deeper experiences in intimacy with others and yourself. Love is healing on all levels of mind body and spirit. This meditation can help you expand your love and fill your experiencing with your love, creating a life with joy.

It is recommended to keep your eyes open for this meditation. Simply focus for a few moments on your 6th illumina surrounding your chest and throat area. Imagine this illumina to be a foot in radius with you as the center. Give yourself a few moments to be in this focus. Then focus on each illumina as indicated below, beginning with the 1st illumina and ending with the 13th illumina.

1st Illumina – (11 feet below your feet)
Focus on this illumina and imagine it expanding to a radius of 2 feet.

2nd Illumina – (4 feet below your feet)
Focus on this illumina and imagine it expanding to a radius of 2 feet.

3rd Illumina – (around your feet)
Focus on this illumina and imagine it expanding to a radius of 2 feet.

4th Illumina – (around your knees)
Focus on this illumina and imagine it expanding to a radius of 2 feet.

5th Illumina – (around your abdomen)
Focus on this illumina and imagine it expanding to a radius of 2 feet.

6th Illumina – (around your chest and throat area)
Focus on this illumina and imagine it expanding to a radius of 2 feet.

7th Illumina – (around your head)
Focus on this illumina and imagine it expanding to a radius of 2 feet.

8th Illumina – (1 foot above head)
Focus on this illumina and imagine it expanding to a radius of 2 feet.

9th Illumina – (2 feet above head)
Focus on this illumina and imagine it expanding to a radius of 2 feet.

10th Illumina – (3 feet above head)
Focus on this illumina and imagine it expanding to a radius of 2 feet.

11th Illumina – (4 feet above head)
Focus on this illumina and imagine it expanding to a radius of 2 feet.

12th Illumina – (5 feet above head)
Focus on this illumina and imagine it expanding to a radius of 2 feet.

13th Illumina – (12 feet above your head)
Focus on this illumina and imagine it expanding to a radius of 2 feet.

Again focus on your 6th illumina surrounding your chest and throat. Imagine the 6th illumina expanding infinitely.
Take a few moments to be still in your energy.

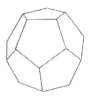

Connecting to Higher Self Meditation

This meditation provides a spiritual experience of connecting to your higher self. We can open to walking every day with the awareness of our higher self and our gifts. We can expand as an individual Divine being of light and love feeling a connection to the oneness of Divine. This meditation offers the opportunity for greater expansion of self, blending all levels of mind, body and spirit.

It is recommended to keep your eyes open for this meditation. Begin the meditation by simply focusing for a few moments on your 6th illumina surrounding your chest and throat area. Imagine the 6th illumina to be a foot in radius with you as the center. Give yourself a few moments to be in the energy of your 6th illumina.

When you feel ready, shift your focus to your 9th light illumina, 2 feet above your head. Imagine the 9th illumina to be a foot in radius with you as the center. Give yourself a few moments to be in the energy of the 9th illumina.

When you feel ready, imagine placing one hand in your 6th illumina and your other hand in your 9th illumina. Take a few moments to still in your energy.

Expanding in Light Meditation

This meditation aligns and balances your energy with your Divine energy. It allows an expansion of your light and your vibration for higher consciousness and awareness. This meditation offers illuminating experiences. After you have completed the last illumina, take a few moments to be still in your energy.

Focus on each light as indicated:

1st Illumina – (11 feet below your feet)
Focus on this Illumina. Close your eyes and imagine golden white healing light. Allow this Illumina to expand through your intention.

2nd Illumina – (4 feet below your feet)
Focus on this Illumina. Close your eyes and imagine golden white healing light. Allow this Illumina to expand through your intention.

3rd Illumina – (around your feet)
Focus on this Illumina. Close your eyes and imagine golden white healing light. Allow this Illumina to expand through your intention.

4th Illumina – (around your knees)
Focus on this Illumina. Close your eyes and imagine golden white healing light. Allow this Illumina to expand through your intention.

5th Illumina – (around your abdomen)
Focus on this Illumina. Close your eyes and imagine golden white healing light. Allow this Illumina to expand through your intention.

6th Illumina – (around your chest and throat area)
Focus on this Illumina. Close your eyes and imagine golden white healing light. Allow this Illumina to expand through your intention.

7th Illumina – (around your head)
Focus on this Illumina. Close your eyes and imagine golden white healing light. Allow this Illumina to expand through your intention.

8th Illumina – (1 foot above head)
Focus on this Illumina. Close your eyes and imagine golden white healing light. Allow this Illumina to expand through your intention.

9th Illumina – (2 feet above head)
Focus on this Illumina. Close your eyes and imagine golden white healing light. Allow this Illumina to expand through your intention.

10th Illumina – (3 feet above head)
Focus on this Illumina. Close your eyes and imagine golden white healing light. Allow this Illumina to expand through your intention.

11th Illumina – (4 feet above head)
Focus on this Illumina. Close your eyes and imagine golden white healing light. Allow this Illumina to expand through your intention.

12th Illumina – (5 feet above head)
Focus on this Illumina. Close your eyes and imagine golden white healing light. Allow this Illumina to expand through your intention.

13th Illumina – (12 feet above your head)
Focus on this Illumina. Close your eyes and imagine golden white healing light. Allow this Illumina to expand through your intention.

Our Illumination

We are spiritual beings; our core essence is love. When we take care of ourselves and give love to ourselves, we can expand the radius of our light. Our light holds the vibration of Divine love.

Our new crystalline light body allows us to hold more of our Divine light. The illuminas give us greater ability to expand and share our light. They provide the opportunity to receive and hold higher vibrational energy to expand our light, open to our Divine abilities, awaken our higher consciousness, open connection with angels and Divine guides, release limitations, and accelerate natural healing. By sharing our light, we can positively affect others, helping them shift in vibration to heal and expand as well.

As we expand our light, we can illuminate the world. Together we can evolve our awareness and spread our light positively influencing the world. Love is the most powerful force and together we can spread love throughout the Earth. This is an exciting time as we move into a new age of illumination. Love and Light to all!

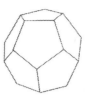

Glossary

Afino- An ascending ople flowing from the 1st illumina to the 13th illumina. The Afino carries Divine light from the descending ople, the Pelo, to circulate the light flowing in the center of the illuminas. This ople makes up part of the Meatus Linaus.

Celfemer- (pronounced chelfmer) A light regulator area located just below the Sea of Light in the 13th illumina. It controls the amount of light flowing into the Pelo, out of the Afino, and through the center of the illuminas.

IJo Ople- A channel of light that makes up part of the Mietor area in the outer edge of our light field. It regulates light that is received from the Divine and others.

Illum- A pentagonal side of the illumina's dodecahedron shape. The dodecahedron shape is made up of a crystalline structure. The illums are energy centers funneling into the center of the illumina. They hold spiritual or physical attributes allowing for opening to and grounding in our spiritual energy.

Illumina- A light center in the light field. There are 13 total illuminas in the light field, each corresponding to different attributes of holding our spiritual self in the Earth plane. They are dodecahedron in shape and crystalline in form. The illuminas are all perfectly and vertically aligned from the 1st illumina located about 11 feet below our feet up to the 13th illumina located about 12 feet above our head. They are our Earth sensors.

Jo ople- A channel of light that makes up the Mietor area in the outer edge of our light field. It regulates light that is emitted from our light body.

Meatus Linaus (Managing Ethereal Alignment To Universal Source, Lineal Intention Nourshing And Unifying Self)- A vertical energetic line running through the center of each of the illuminas and our physical body. It is made up of the Afino and Pelo oples, two channels of Divine light flowing upward and downward with continuous flow. It runs from the 12th illumina down to the 1st, then back up to the 13th illumina.

Mietor (Managing Internal and External Transmission of Radiance)- The outermost edge of our newly evolving crystalline light body (field). It is made up of two oples, the Jo ople and IJo ople. It regulates the transmission of our spiritual light in two ways: how much of our spiritual light is being emitted, managed by the Jo ople, and how much light is being received from Divine and others, managed by the IJo ople.

Oples- The channels of light within and around the light field.

Pelo- A descending ople flowing from the 13th illumina to the 1st illumina. The Pelo carries Divine light to the ascending ople, the Afino, to circulate the light flowing in the center of the illuminas. This ople makes up part of the Meatus Linaus.

Sea of Light- A light regulator area located in the lower part of the 13th illumina. Light is regulated through the Pelo and Afino oples. This is a neo-plasmic field that holds energetic light information.

This information can be accessed and utilized when needed for this Earth experience.

Uepo (pronounced: oo-way-po)- The Source light channel located on the upper part of the 13th illumina. It regulates the amount of Divine light flowing through the Sea of Light into the illuminas.

Printed in the United States
By Bookmasters